A Condensed Santeria Guide for Beginners

A Brief Beginners Guide to Santeria History, Practices, Deities, Spells and Rituals

By Riley Star

Foreword

The word "Santeria" is translated from the Spanish for "worship of saints", though that translation alone doesn't really paint an accurate picture of what Santeria is all about. Not only does Santeria involve the worship of saints (called Orishas), but it is also a quest for enlightenment and kinship with God. What makes Santeria so unique is the fact that it is a syncretic religion – it combines the beliefs and practices of several religions, primarily the African Yoruba religion with Roman Catholic elements mixed in.

While Santeria originated in the Caribbean, it has been spread throughout the world. Unfortunately, however, there is still a great deal of controversy and misunderstanding surrounding the practice of Santeria. If you are curious to learn more about this religion – and if you want to learn the truth behind the myths – this book is the perfect place for you to begin. By the time you finish this book you will have a thorough understanding of what Santeria is and how it is practiced. So, if you are ready to start learning, just turn the page and keep reading!

Table of Contents

Introduction

When it comes to religion you can probably name most of the big players – Christianity, Catholicism, Judaism, Hinduism, Islam, Buddhism, and so on. But what about the smaller religions? The religions that have existed for centuries, yet many people remain unaware that they exist. One of these religions that often escapes notice but is actually widely practiced is called Santeria, a syncretic religion that originated in the Caribbean and was developed in West Africa.

People who practice Santeria prefer to use the name Regla de Ocha, though the word "Santeria" is actually translated from the Spanish for "worship of saints". What makes Santeria so unique is the fact that it is a syncretic religion – it combines the beliefs and practices of several religions. You will notice that much of the terminology used in Santeria overlaps with terminology and concepts taken from Catholicism in addition to its West African influences – this is an example of religious syncretism.

While Santeria originated in the Caribbean, it has been spread throughout the world. Unfortunately, however, there is still a great deal of controversy and misunderstanding surrounding the practice of Santeria. If you are curious to learn more about this religion – and if you want to learn the truth behind the myths – this book is the perfect place for you to begin. Within the pages of this book you will find an introduction to Santeria and its core concepts as well as the history of the religion and its spread throughout the world. You will also receive in-depth information about Santeria beliefs and practices as well as information about performing rituals.

By the time you finish this book you will have a thorough understanding of what Santeria is and how it is practiced. So, if you are ready to start learning, just turn the page and keep reading!

Useful Terms to Know

Aborisha – A term given to the individual worshipper as well as the worship of the Orisha.

Addimu – Cooked foods given as token offerings of love and thanks to the Orishas or to the ancestors.

Ayé - The name given to the physical realm in Santeria religion.

Divination – The practice of seeking knowledge of the future or the unknown by supernatural means.

Guerreros - Warriors; a type of initiation during which the santero receives several Orishas - Echu Elegguá, Ogún, Ochossi, and Osun.

Ebó – A ritual sacrifice or offering as dictated through divination; they take many forms including ritual baths, fresh fruit offerings, animal sacrifice, and initiations.

Eyebale – The name given to a blood sacrifice; typically performed with chickens, roosters, sheep, goats, or pigeons.

Ilekes - Necklaces; a type of initiation during which the santero comes under the blessing and protection of the godparents' Orishas.

Initiation - A series of ceremonies and rituals during which an individual invokes their tutelary Orisha.

Isoguí – A form of Ebó that consists of the Orisha's favorite fresh fruits.

Iyawo - A newly initiated santero.

Kariocha - A week-long initiation in which a santero becomes a priest or priestess of the Santeria religion.

La Regla Lukumi – Another name used for the Santeria religion.

Odu - The letters or signs that appear during divination using diloggún (cowrie shells) or an epuele (a divining chain) used by a Babalawo.

Olorisha - Another name for practitioners of Santeria.

Olorun - Also known as Olodumare, the supreme deity and creator of the universe; God.

Omiero - A liquid made from a variety of herbs, each with properties that correspond to a specific Orisha.

Orisha – A spiritual being or presence interpreted as one of the manifestations of God.

Patakis - Sacred stories used to teach Santeria values; each one is correlated with a specific Orisha.

Proverbs - Stories that have been passed down orally from one generation to the next; each one is connected to an odu.

Regla de Ocha – Translates to *The Rule of the Orisha*, another name for Santeria.

Religious Syncretism - A melding of religious practices.

Sacrifice - An offering given to the Orishas, often in the form of an animal blood sacrifice.

Saint – A person acknowledged as holy or virtuous and typically regarded as being in heaven after death.

Santeria – Translates to The Way of the Saints; a syncretic religion with African origins and Spanish influence.

Santero - A practioner of Santeria.

Syncretism - See Religious Syncretism.

Yoruba - An ancient African people found primarily in Nigeria as well as adjoining parts of Togo and Benin; this area is collectively referred to as Yorubaland.

Chapter One: What is Santeria?

When you hear the word Santeria it may bring to mind the 90s song written by Sublime that opens with the line, "I don't practice Santeria". Aside from that, however, you may not know anything about Santeria at all unless you have done some research of your own or taken a world religion class. Though many people assume that Santeria is a small, localized religion it is actually widely practiced around the world. Santeria, at its most basic level, is an African way of worship that features many Catholic elements. In this chapter you will learn the basics about what Santeria is, where it is practiced, and its history.

1.) Where is Santeria Practiced?

There is conflicting information out there regarding the exact origins of the Santeria religion, but it is generally known to have Caribbean origins and that it was developed in the Spanish Empire. Some say that the home of Santeria is Cuba, though it is widely practiced throughout the Spanish-speaking world. Some of the countries known to still practice Santeria include Cuba, the Dominican Republic, Puerto Rico, Panama, Venezuela, Colombia, and Mexico. There are even parts of the United States where the religion is regularly practiced.

A study conducted in the early 2000s revealed an estimated 22,000 practitioners of Santeria in the United

States alone, though the number could be much higher in reality. Santerian practices have taken a lot of heat in the United States, especially things like animal sacrifice. This issue was taken to the United States Supreme Court in 1993 in the case of Church of Lukumi Babalu Aye v. City of Hialeah. The ruling of the court decided that animal cruelty laws which specifically targeted Santeria and its practices were unconstitutional.

2.) Why is it Called Santeria?

The name Santeria translates from the Spanish word that means "worship of saints". For many practitioners of Santeria, however, the religion has a different name – *La Regla Lukumi* or *the Rule of Osha*. As a religion, Santeria combines various concepts and terminology from other world religions including Catholicism and various West African religions – this melding of religious practices is known as religious syncretism.

Santeria involves the worship of the Orisha – this translates to mean "head guardians" and it refers to a spiritual being or presence that can be interpreted as a manifestation of God. The Orisha are considered lesser guardians, a step below the god Olorun, the supreme deity and creator of the universe. The practice of Santeria is based on the development of a personal relationship between the practitioner (called olorishas) and various deities through various rituals and sacrifices.

3.) *The History of Santeria*

Santeria is technically an Afro-Caribbean religion that grew out of the Cuban slave trade. It is primarily an oral tradition that is centered on various African traditions but parallels some aspects of Catholicism and other Western religions. Santeria (sometimes translated to mean "the way of the saints") is based on Yoruba beliefs and traditions. The Yoruba people are found primarily in Nigeria as well as the adjoining parts of Togo and Benin – this area is collectively referred to as Yorubaland.

The Yoruba religion is an ancient one and its beliefs are part of itan, the name for the group of cultural concepts which dictate Yoruban society. One of the core beliefs of the Yoruba people is that each person possesses an "Ayanmo", a destiny or fate, and they are expected to eventually become one with the divine creator, Olorun. They also believe that the actions and thoughts of each individual person in the physical realm (called Aye) interact with and affect all living things, even the Earth itself. Through various rituals and practices, the individual strengthens his relationship with Olorun in an attempt to find his destiny and to achieve transcendence.

When the slave trade began, Yoruba slaves brought their religion with them to the Western world. In an effort to preserve their beliefs and practices, they found ways to merge their religious customs with certain aspects of Roman

Catholicism. This syncretic religion evolved into what is known as modern day Santeria. To give you an idea of what this looked like, consider this quote from Ernesto Pichardo from his book *Santeria in Contemporary Cuba: The Individual Life and Condition of the Priesthood*:

> The colonial period from the standpoint of African slaves may be defined as a time of perseverance. Their world quickly changed. Tribal kings and their families, politicians, business and community leaders all were enslaved and taken to a foreign region of the world. Religious leaders, their relatives and their followers were now slaves. Colonial laws criminalized their religion. They were forced to become baptized and worship a god their ancestors had not known who was surrounded by a pantheon of saints.

> The early concerns during this period seem to have necessitated a need for individual survival under harsh plantation conditions. A sense of hope was sustaining the internal essence of what today is called Santería, a misnomer (and former pejorative) for the indigenous religion of the Lukumi people of Nigeria. In the heart of their homeland, they had a complex political and social order. They were a sedentary hoe farming cultural group with specialized labor. Their religion, based on the worship of nature, was renamed and documented by their masters.

> Santería, a pejorative term that characterizes deviant Catholic forms of worshiping saints, has become a common name for the religion. The term santero(a) is used to describe a priest or priestess replacing the traditional term Olorisha as an extension of the deities. The orishas became known as the saints in image of the Catholic pantheon.

For many years, Santeria was something of an underground religion. In fact, it was once dismissed as a "ghetto religion" only practiced by the Caribbean poor and uneducated. In recent years, however, Santeria has grown among the middle class and it is becoming increasingly visible throughout the Americas. Still, it is difficult to say how many people practice Santeria because there is no central organization and it is a religion typically practiced in private. There are some who estimate as many as 100 million practitioners worldwide.

Chapter Two: Getting to Know Santeria

Santeria is sometimes difficult for newcomers to understand because on one level it is a very personal and private experience while, on another level, it is a communal and largely tribal religion. In this chapter you will learn a little bit more about who practices Santeria, what they are called, and what the initiation process looks like. It is important to remember that there is no one set path to initiation in the religion of Santeria and not everyone is destined to become fully initiated. Keep reading to learn more about what initiation looks like and the different kinds of initiations that come into play.

1.) Who Practices Santeria?

People who practice Santeria are generally known as santeros, though the term "aborisha" may also be used. Santeros practice Santeria by worshiping Olorun (also known as Olodumare), the supreme being and creator of the universe, as well as the Orishas (the saints). In exchange for submission to their deities, santeros are promised supernatural powers and protection from evil – this includes good health, position, influence, and the ability to see and modify the future.

People who practice Santeria believe in reincarnation – that a person's destiny is already decided before birth – and, through rituals and sacrifices, they can determine which actions to take which will propel them toward enlightenment and toward their destiny. These practices also enable the santero to receive commands from the Orishas that they are required to obey.

2.) Santeria Deities

Santeria is a religion that focuses on building a relationship between humans and Orishas. Orishas as powerful spirits, a mortal manifestation of God (called Olodumare). Followers of the Santeria religion believe that the Orishas will guide them through life, enabling them to achieve their destiny, as long as they carry out specific rituals and offer sacrifices. It is a symbiotic relationship – the

Orishas need to be worshipped in order to continue existing and humans need the Orishas to meet their ultimate destiny.

There are many misconceptions out there about the Santeria religion and one of them regards the idea of Santeria being a pagan religion. This confusion may stem from the fact that Orishas are often referred to as Gods which could suggest that Santeria is a polytheistic religion similar to paganism. In reality, however, Santeria understands the Orishas as different aspects of the one God (Olodumare) as they are manifested in the physical world. Like many modern religions, Santeria only believes in one true God.

Every follower of Santeria has his or her own destiny as decided by Olodumare. Each person is also thought to be the child of a specific Orisha of which there are hundreds. When an individual is initiated into the Santeria religion, he or she must first appeal to the Orishas in order to determine their path and to solidify their commitment to their tutelary Orisha. That Orisha will then guide them throughout their lives in their journey toward enlightenment.

Though there are many different Orishas in the Santeria religion, certain ones are more commonly worshipped than others. Each Orisha can be correlated with a specific saint in the Roman Catholic religion, and they are also correlated with certain colors and numbers which come into play during rituals and ceremonies.

The Orishas that are most commonly worshipped include the following:

Eleggua	Eleva, Elegba
Saint: Saint Anthony	
Number: 3, 21	
Color: Red and black	
Notes: The first and most important Orisha. He is the owner of crossroads, the witness of fates, and acts as a connecting agent in the world.	
Ogún	**Oggún**
Saint: Saint Peter	
Number: 3	
Color: Green and black	
Notes: A mighty warrior and divine blacksmith who makes tools and weapons – the hardest working Orisha and the father of technology.	
Ochosi	**Ochossi, Oshosi**
Saint: Saint Norbert	

Number: 3, 7	
Color: Blue and amber	
Notes: The divine hunter whose arrow never misses its mark. He is the force of blind justice that is applied equally to all.	
Orisha Oko	**Orichaoco**
Saint: Saint Isidore	
Number: 7	
Color: Light blue and pink	
Notes: The Orisha of agriculture and fertile earth, he rules the mystery of black earth that gives life to crops – also the Orisha of fertility and procreation.	
Olokun	
Saint: None	
Number: 9	
Color: Dark blue with green	
Notes: The Orisha that rules the depths of the sea where light doesn't touch. He is mysterious and it is unknown whether he is male or female.	
Babalú Ayé	**Babaluaye, Asojano**
Saint: Saint Lazarus	

Number: 17	
Color: White, blue, brown, black	
Notes: One of the most beloved and worshipped Orishas, the Orisha of contagious disease and healing. He is depicted as an old man covered in sores, walking on crutches and accompanied by two dogs.	
Ibeji	**Ibeyi, Ibelli, Melli**
Saint: Saint Cosme and Saint Damian	
Number: 2, 4 and 8	
Color: Red and blue	
Notes: The divine twins, they are considered one Orisha. The twins are sacred to the Lukumi people – they are the children of Oshún and Changó.	
Obatalá	
Saint: Our Lady of Mercy	
Number: 8	
Color: White	
Notes: The eldest of the Orishas, the owner of white cloth and king of peace and logic. He mediates disputes between other Orishas and encourages the use of diplomacy and reason.	
Obba	

Saint: Saint Catherine of Siena

Number: 8

Color: Brown, opal and coral

Notes: The Orisha of marriage and personal transformation. She was Shangó's wife who was shunned and fled to the cemetery where she underwent a transformational journey to discover her true power.

Oyá	Yansa, Yansan

Saint: Our Lady of Candelmas or Saint Theresa

Number: 9

Color: Brown, dark red, or multi-color

Notes: A fierce female warrior and the Orisha of change. She scares away death (Ikú) and is the owner of the cemetery gates.

Yeguá	Yewá

Saint: Our Lady of Montserrat

Number: 7, 9

Color: Pink and burgundy

Notes: The special daughter of Oduduwa and once a symbol of purity and chastity. Her purity was tainted when violated by Changó and has become the Orisha linked to death and the dying process.

Aggayú	Agajú, Aganyu
Saint: Saint Christopher	
Number: 9	
Color: Brown and opal	
Notes: The father of Shangó and the Orisha of the volcano and ferryman who takes people across the river.	

Ochún	Oshún
Saint: Our Lady of Charity and Cobre	
Number: 5	
Color: Yellow and amber	
Notes: The Orisha of sweetness, love, and beauty – the embodiment of feminine grace and a flirtatious coquette. She is a loving and generous mother but can turn bitter quickly if wronged.	

Yemayá	Yemoja
Saint: Our Lady of Regla	
Number: 7	
Color: Blue and clear	
Notes: The mother of all living things, queen of heaven and earth. She lives in the ocean and she is the mother of many children and other Orishas.	

Shangó	Changó, Sango
Saint: Saint Barbara	
Number: 6	
Color: Red and white	
Notes: The king of the Santeria religion and once the fourth king of the city of Oyó in Yorubaland before he was defied and thus became an Orisha.	
Orunmila	**Orunla, Orula**
Saint: Saint Francis of Assisi	
Number: 16	
Color: Yellow and green (or brown and green)	
Notes: The Orisha of divination and the patron of the Ifá sect. Along with Elegguá, he witnessed all of destiny unfold and can help a person determine their fate.	

3.) Initiation Rituals and Paths

The road to initiation within the Santeria religion looks different for every individual. It can be influenced by the godparent you choose and by your own personal destiny. The initiation process is designed to help you learn about Santeria and to determine your individual path. Though there are many directions an initiation can take, the first step is usually divination. There are two types of divination – Ifa and Diloggún. Each divination has the potential to turn up 256 different signs which will give you a reading of your past, present, and future. A divination will help to show you which path to take.

With guidance from the Orishas, divination will help you to determine what kind of initiation to complete. <u>Here is an overview of some of the many Santeria initiations</u>:

- **Guerreros (Warriors)** – During this initiation you will receive several Orishas (Echu Elegguá, Ogún, Ochossi, and Osun). These Orishas will be placed by your front door and you must care for them and work with them.

- **Ilekes or Collares** – Receiving your Ilekes, or necklaces, will put you under the blessing and protection of your godparents' Orishas, making you a part of their Orisha House (or Ilé). Preparations for this ceremony are very complex and can take several takes to complete and the ceremony itself can take several ours because it is made up of several rites.

- **Mano de Orula** – This initiation means "Hand of Orula" and it is an initiation into the world of Ifá, putting you under the protection of Orula. For men, this ceremony is called Awofakan and, for women, it is called Ikofá.

- **Olokun from Ocha** – Receiving Olokun (a very powerful and mysterious Orisha) can add depth to an individual's spirituality and help him make a stronger connection with his ancestors.

- **Ibeji (the twins)** – For people who are destined to receive the Ibeji, they should receive Elegguá first. Receving the Ibeji can help the individual to fend off negative obstructions in their life.

- **Addimu Orisha** – On rare occasions, divination will reveal a need for a particular Orisha to help guide his path and protect him from misfortunes (called osogbo). Receiving an Orisha outside of the kariocha ceremony is referred to as the reception of an Addimu Orisha.

- **Kariocha** – This is the most powerful initiation in the Santeria religion and the name kariocha means "to seat the orisha". Only people who are marked for kariocha through divination can receive this initiation and it is a large ceremony that takes place over a seven-day period and involves many priests and priestesses. Before starting the ceremony, the individual's tutelary Orisha must be determined through divination.

- **Pinaldo** – This ceremony can be performed after an individual has been made a priest or priestess through kariocha. Pinaldo is a ceremony that involves animal sacrifice to make the individual's Ogun full.

- **Making Ifá** – If a person is not destined to be made an Ocha, they may be initiated as a Babalawo (or Father of the Secrets) to specialize in the deepest forms of divination. This is considered the highest form of priesthood.

Each initiation ceremony is different but there are some common rituals which are typically involved. <u>Some of the most common rituals used in Santeria initiations include the following</u>:

- **Divination** – As you have already learned, divination must be performed prior to initiation in order to determine the individual's path of destiny.

- **Derecho/Ashedi** – Every initiation in the Santeria religion has an associated cost called a derecho or ashedi. While the practice of paying for initiation is not common in Western religions, it is a common practice in traditional African culture and religion. The ashedi is put towards the cost of supplies required for the initiation – herbs, tools, animals, food, clothes, etc. – and a portion is given to the godparents and olorishas who work the ceremony.

- **Animal Sacrifice** – Every initiation in the Santeria religion requires some form of animal sacrifice because initiation is a rebirth, an entry into a new life and a new destiny.

- **Taboos/Restrictions** – During initiation, many Santeria newcomers are required to enter a period of observed restrictions and taboos to help keep their energy pure and to ensure a greater sacred experience. The longest period of taboo occurs after the kariocha initiation – it lasts a full year during which the participant must wear all white.

Now that you have a deeper understanding of the different initiations and practices they involve you are ready to learn a little more about the specific beliefs and practices involved in Santeria. In the next chapter you will receive an overview of Santeria deities, rituals, and customs as well as information about Santeria proverbs, sacrifices, and offerings.

Chapter Three: Beliefs and Practices

On the whole, Santeria is a religion that focuses on building a relationship between humans and the Orishas. Santeria is a very ritualistic religion with specific initiations and practices that must be performed at certain times and in certain ways. In this chapter you will learn a little more about Santeria deities, rituals, and customs and you will receive an overview of important information regarding Santeria proverbs, sacrifices, and offerings. This chapter will help to deepen your understanding of the Santeria religion as a whole.

1.) Santeria Patakis

In many ways, Santeria is an oral religion and the sacred stories used to teach Santeria values are called "patakis". These stories have been passed down from one generation to the next for thousands of years and each ilé may have a slightly different way of telling the story, though the central message remains the same. It is traditional for specific patakis to be linked to specific odu, the letters or signs that appear during divination using diloggún (cowrie shells) or an epuele (a divining chain) used by a Babalawo.

When it comes to interpreting a reading, there is no written codex of meanings – the Santero must memorize as much information as they can about each odu and a certain degree of interpretive skill is needed to determine the subtle and complex message each odu provides in correlation to the individual client's situation. Patakis linked to each odu help the diviner remember key information about that odu which they can then use to understand the message of the reading and relate it to the client.

Patakis frequently tell stories about the Orishas, talking about their lives on earth, their interactions with humans and with each other, and their relationship to God. Some patakis also serve to explain various fundamental principles of the Santeria religion, such as the connection of specific elements (like thunder, lightning, rivers, or mountains) with specific Orishas. Patakis explain the preference of each Orisha for specific foods (which comes into play with ritual sacrifices) and they help to explain the origins of certain customs and ceremonies.

You do not have to be a diviner to learn and retell the patakis. In order to fully grasp the meaning of the story as well as its complex implications, however, you need a certain degree of knowledge and training in interpreting the odu. It is only fully initiated priests and priestesses who can read the diloggún and only Babalawos are allowed to work with the epuele. Becoming skilled in diloggún interpretation takes many years of study and not all santeros are destined for that line of work. In most cases, santeros have a general knowledge of patakis but deep knowledge of patakis is optional in most communities.

2.) *Santeria Proverbs*

Another device commonly used in the Santeria religion that is similar to patakis are the proverbs. In the same way that each Pataki is connected to specific odu, each odu is connected to specific proverbs. These proverbs have been established through many years of custom and tradition and they too are passed down orally from one generation to the next. The exact number of proverbs in existence is unknown because different ilés know different proverbs for each odu. Learning as many proverbs as possible will help to increase your skill as a diviner.

Similar to patakis, proverbs can be used to interpret odu, helping to attach a deeper metaphorical meaning that the individual client can then apply to his life. They can also be used as a kind of mnemonic device to help the diviner remember the meaning of certain odus. For example, the proverb "with the tongue you can save or destroy the town" is connected to the odu Obara which reminds the client about the power of his tongue to do either great harm or great god.

To give you an idea of the connection between different proverbs and various odus, here is a list of common Santeria proverbs and their general meanings:

- **"He who gives bread to someone else's dog loses the bread and loses the dog."** (*El que da pan al perro ajeno, pierde el pan y pierde el perro.*) This proverb is a reminder of the fine line between the desire to help someone and the need to interfere with their business. Even with the best of intentions, it is easy to overstep boundaries and to get involved in situations we have no business getting involved in.

- **"The Devil knows more because he's old, not because he's the devil."** (*Más sabe el diablo por Viejo que por diablo.*) This proverb is borrowed from Spanish culture because there is no devil in the Lukumi religion. This proverb reminds us that knowledge is acquired over time and that patience and humility are required to gain wisdom.

- **"Human beings disapprove of things they can't achieve."** (*El hombre desaprueba lo que no puede realizer.*) This proverb touches on envy and frustration as well as the importance of knowing your rightful place. Not everyone is meant to be a leader and you will find the greatest satisfaction in fulfilling the role you were destined to fill.

Now that you have a better understanding of how to interpret Santeria proverbs, give it a try for yourself with these proverbs:

- **"Good character is the essence of beauty."** (*Buen caracter is la esencia de la belleza.*)
- **"The shrimp that falls asleep gets taken by the current."** (*Camarron que se duerme se lo lleva la corriente.*)
- **"A dog has four legs, yet can only choose one trail."** (*El perro tiene quatro patas y coge un solo camino.*)
- **"He is so happy ignorant that it will be a pity, when he opens his senses."** (*El es feliz ignorante, pero pobre de el cuando habran sus sentidos.*)

- **"Look for evil in your own home."** (*El mal busquelo en su casa.*)
- **"Gratitude is memory within the heart."** (*El agradecimiento es la memoria del Corazon.*)
- **"Whom was born to be a head cannot be a tail."** (*El que nacio para cabeza, no puede ser cola.*)
- **"Matrimony is a palace with two doors, a true one and a false one."** (*El matrimonio es un palacio de dos puertas, la verdardera, y la falsa.*)
- **"You can't know what is love if you are not in love."** (*No sabe lo que es amor, aquel que no esta enamorado.*)
- **"He who does not know is like he who does not see."** (*El que no sabe es como el que no ve.*)
- **"It is best to eat a little bit everyday than to eat much for only one day."** (*Es mejor comer poco todos los dia, que comer mucho una sola vez.*)
- **"The mind is for thinking, the eyes for seeing, the ears for hearing, yet all that you think, see, and hear should not be said."** (*La cerebro is para pensar, los ojos para ver, los oido para oir, pero no todo lo que se sabe, se oye, y se ve, se puede hablar.*)
- **"He who commits adultery with the wife of a man will always be his enemy."** (*El que comete adulterior con la esposa de un hombre siempre sera su enemigo.*)
- **"There are those that live in the dark, even when the sun surrounds them with light."** (*Hay quien vive en la oscuridad aun cuando Olorun lo rodea con luz.*)

- **"When your head is on your shoulders, your thoughts fixed on the horizon, and feet in salt water, no doubt we're facing the ocean."** (*Cuando la cabeza se tiene sobre los hombros, el pensamiento hacia el horizonte, nuestros pies en agua salada, no cabe duda que estamos frente al mar.*)
- **"The eyes of mankind can only see God through tears."** (*Los Ojos del hombre solamente ven a Olodumare entre lagrimas.*)

3.) Santeria Rituals and Sacrifices

According to Merriam-Webster, a ritual is defined as, "done as part of a ceremony" or "according to religious law". Santeria is a very ritualistic religion and rituals are the methods santeros use to remain connected to their Orishas. These rituals may include various forms of dancing, speaking, drumming, and even eating with the Orishas. These rituals usually take place in halls that are rented specifically for that purpose or in the homes of priests and priestesses which are filled with altars designed for specific ritualistic purposes.

Most Santeria rituals begin with the invocation of Olorun with drums being beaten to African rhythms. As the ritual continues, the rhythm (called the Oru) changes to a beat that is associated with a specific Orisha who is then invoked. Another important aspect of many Santeria rituals is the animal sacrifice. Chickens are the animals most commonly used during ritual sacrifices and, in most cases, the blood of the animal is collected and offered to the Orisha. These sacrifices are believed to please the Orishas, bringing good luck as well as purification and forgiveness for sins.

The term "Ebó" is given to ritual offerings or sacrifices in the Santeria religion and they take many forms ranging from ritual baths to offerings of fresh fruits or animal sacrifice. Animal sacrifices are carried out in a very specific way in the Santeria religion. The animal is offered up to the Orisha and then its carotid artery is severed with a single knife stroke. After the blood is collected and offered up to the Orisha, the animal is cooked and eaten in an act that is considered sharing with the Orisha – the Orisha only consumes the blood while the humans consume the flesh. The only rituals where animal sacrifices are not eaten is healing and death rites because the sickness of the human is believed to be passed to the dead animal.

4.) Omiero – Types and Preparation

   Santeria is a highly ceremonial religion that involves many rituals. One of the most important rituals involved in the Santeria religion is the initiation. There are many different types of initiation depending on the individual's tutelary Orisha, but they all begin with divination to determine the individual's path. Once the individual's Orisha has been determined, he must be initiated to that

Orisha through a specific ceremony which typically involves some form of sacrifice.

Most Santeria sacrifices involve the blood and flesh of animals, but during the initiation itself, the practitioner uses a sacred liquid called Omiero rather than blood. Omiero is a liquid made from a variety of herbs, each with properties that correspond to a specific Orisha. During the initiation ceremony, the Omiero is used to pathe the initiate (the Iyawo) and to wash the Otan (stones) which are consecrated to the Orishas. It may also be used in purification rituals.

Each Orisha linked to specific herbs and ingredients, so there are many different types of Omiero. It is important to note that while different herbs can be linked to specific Orishas, they also represent taboo for other Orishas – that is why it is so important to use exactly the right ingredients when preparing an Omiero for an initiation or purification ceremony. Some of the herbs used in Omiero may include:

- Azowano
- Aña Oath
- Jimaguas (Ibeyis)
- Obatala
- Ochun
- Odduduwa
- Orunmila
- Oggún

- Orisha Oko
- Orumila and Orun
- Oshosi and Osun
- Oya and Shango
- Yemaya

As is true for many aspects of the Santeria religion, the exact herbs and preparation methods for Omiero are kept secret, even to the initiates. Throughout their initiation, it is very common for new practitioners of Santeria to hear that they are not allowed to know the details of the ceremony – it is something they must learn in time as they delve deeper into their relationship with the Orishas in their quest for enlightenment.

Chapter Four: The Secrecy of Santeria

     If you head to your local library in search of a Santeria guide book, you probably won't find it. You might find a reference book that includes mention of Santeria and other African-derived religions but, if you were hoping to find details about Santeria rituals and ceremonies, you shouldn't get your hopes up. Santeria is a highly secretive religion. Even when individuals are going through the initiation process, the details of the ritual are not disclosed – it takes years for a santero to receive these details. In this chapter you will find some tips for learning more about Santeria if you are considering initiation.

1.) Why is Santeria Such a Secretive Religion?

Santeria is a highly ritualistic and ceremonial religion and while Santeria rituals do follow specific guidelines and involve the use of certain herbs, songs, dances, and more, the details are only known by priests, priestesses, and others who have been following the practice of Santeria for many years. But why is Santeria such a secretive religion? It all goes back to the history of Santeria and its African origins prior to the advent of the slave trade.

As you may remember from the history section of this book, Santeria is a religion derived from the Yoruba tradition with various Roman Catholic influences. When Yoruba slaves were brought to the new world, they brought their religious customs and traditions with them. When they arrived in the new world, however, they were expected to accept the religion of their new world which, at the time, was Roman Catholicism. In an effort to preserve their traditions and their beliefs, they incorporated various aspects of Catholicism into a new religious tradition that became known as Santeria.

Because the beliefs and traditions of Santeria are so different from those of the largest Western religions, practitioners kept their beliefs and their rituals secret as a means of self-preservation. Certain practices like animal sacrifice and worship of idols was highly frowned upon so they could not be performed out in the open. This level of secrecy, along with the Santeria traditions themselves, has been passed down through the generations and the secrecy itself has become its own tradition, in a way.

2.) Where Can You Go for Information?

Unlike Christianity which has the Bible as a guide for practitioners, Santeria does not have a written account of its teachings – it is a largely oral tradition that is passed down from one generation to the next. This being the case, you may not be able to find a great deal of literature about Santeria – your best bet for information is to connect with a local church or, at the very least, to speak to a priest or priestess in your area who has completed the initiation process into the religion.

Santeria is a complex religion and the fact that it is highly secretive means that there is no structured path set forth in some kind of guide book. Each person's experience with Santeria is completely unique – it will be shaped by the godparent(s) they choose, the Orisha they invoke, and the type of initiation they go through. Because Santeria is so complex a religion, you should not rush the process of learning about it and of determining whether it is a good fit for you or not.

If you are seriously considering joining the Santeria religion, here are some tips for how to go about it:

- Do some reading to learn the basics about the religion – in addition to this book you may want to try John Mason's *Four New World Yoruba Rituals* and Tobe Melora Correals *Finding Soul on the Path to the Orisha*.

You may also be able to find other books online or at your local library.

- Ask around and find yourself some godparents (or a single godparent). Remember, not everyone is destined for full initiation so you do not necessarily have to find a priest or priestess for information and guidance.

- Spend as much time as you can with your godparent, learning the ins and outs of Santeria through hands-on experience.

- Don't be afraid to ask questions and be open to learning whatever your godparent has to teach you – just be careful about asking for too many details because you won't get them. If you ask too many questions of an elder you also run the risk of offending them.

- If you don't feel a connection with your godparent, don't be afraid to look for another one – it is very important to find a godparent you connect with before you go through initiation and enter their ile (house).

- Once you have chosen your godparent, start attending events of the ile – many events are open to non-initiates and they are a great place to learn about the Santeria religion.

- Go through the ceremony to receive your elekes when you are ready to join an ile – this is the first ceremony most people go through, but not all.

- Go through the divination process to determine your path – if initiation is your destiny, your godparent and your ile will help you achieve that goal. You can also learn about your tutelary Orisha through the process of divination.

Remember, each person's path in the Santeria religion is different and it is a matter of destiny – you do not get to choose your path, but you can choose whether or not to follow it. If you think that initiation is the right path for you, you will find information about what to expect in the next section.

3.) What to Expect When Initiating Into Santeria

Although Santeria is a religion that is commonly practiced in private by the individual, it is not something you can just pick up on your own. It takes a great deal of time to learn Santeria and you need the guidance of a priest to help you learn the practices. One thing you need to know before you start the initiation process is that it is not a quick transition – the road to enlightenment through Santeria is a long, steady walk and not a race. You should also know that there is no clearly defined finish line. Some people are destined to go all the way to priesthood while others are destined to fulfill certain roles within the community.

If you do successfully complete initiation, it will take you a year and one week. During the first week of initiation you will go through a number of ceremonies and you must adhere to certain rules and principles. After that first week, your initiation continues for a full year during which you must wear only white and avoid contact with any non-initiates. You are not allowed to drink alcohol, to shave or wear makeup, or to eat with other practitioners at the same table. You must not go out after dark, shake hands or hug anyone who has not been initiated, and you are not permitted to visit crowded places.

All of these rules and more are designed to keep the initiate pure for the ceremonies and to ensure that they devote their time to understanding and implementing the advice of the Orisha. At the end of your initiation year you will be reborn and, as a newly initiated santero (called an Iyawo). It is important to remember, however, that not everyone completes initiation successfully – it is up to the Orishas whether or not an individual is destined to be initiated. The initiation process is full of ceremonies, rituals, and divinations that build upon each other to help determine the Orisha's will for the individual.

Before you can start the initiation process, you must connect with a godparent, a priest or priestess who has been initiated as an Olorisha. This is not a process you should rush, either. Take the time (it could take weeks or months) to really get to know your godparent and to determine whether or not it is a good fit. This is the person who will be leading you through the long initiation process so you need to find someone with whom you have a good connection. Remember, Santeria is a communal religion with a tribal core, so you must be able to connect and work with everyone in your godfamily.

Once you have connected with a godparent, he or she will lead you through the process of divination – a diloggún reading – which will help you to determine what your destiny is and where your path through the Santeria religion lies. It is important to remember that initiation is not within every person's destiny – this reading will help to tell you whether or not this is the case. If initiation is in your destiny, you will learn the religion through apprenticeship with your godparent.

As you complete your initiation, you will learn primarily through observation. At first you may be required to perform seemingly menial tasks like taking out the garbage, plucking chickens, or sweeping the floor. Instead of viewing these tasks as meaningless, however, you should take the time to experience the sanctity of service toward others. Even though these tasks may seem silly, they are just as important as the role played by the Oriaté in singing the songs for various rituals – if you don't complete your tasks, the ritual cannot be completed.

Chapter Five: Comparing Santeria to Other African Religions

By now you should have a deeper understanding of the Santeria religion and what makes it unique. But how does it compare to other religions, particularly other African-derived religions? In this chapter you will receive an overview of how Santeria compares and contrasts with other similar religions. This will help you to cultivate a more thorough understanding of what Santeria is and what it is not.

1.) Voodoo, Hoodoo, and Santeria

As you already know, Santeria is an African-derived religion. Due to this fact, it is commonly confused with other African Diasporic Traditions such as Voodoo and Hoodoo. Many people who have a poor understanding of African religion use the term "Voodoo" very loosely but it actually refers to a specific set of beliefs and traditions. It is also important to note that Hoodoo is something else entirely and that both religions differ from Santeria in a number of important ways. <u>In the following pages you will find an overview of Voodoo and Hoodoo to help you understand what these differences are:</u>

Santeria

Overview of Voodoo

The religion that many people know of as Voodoo is actually spelled Vodou or Vodoun by practitioners of the religion. It is an African Diasporic Religion that originated in Haiti but currently has two branches – Haitian Vodou and Louisiana (specifically New Orleans) Vodoun. Followers of Haitian Vodou believe in a supreme creator known as Bondye and they worship his servant spirits called Ioa. Similar to Santeria Orishas, each Ioa is connected to a specific aspect of life and each follower connects with a particular Ioa who becomes his guide. Followers of Haitian Vodou present offerings to their Ioa and build altars – there are also many traditional ceremonies and rituals.

Louisiana Vodoun is also known as New Orleans Voodoo and it differs from Haitian Vodou primarily in its emphasis on Voodoo Queens, called gris-gris. These Voodoo queens were responsible for leading ceremonies and rituals, drawing huge crowds of people – they typically made a living selling and administering their charms, amulets, and magical powders. In the same way that Santeria was blended with Spanish Catholicism, Voodoo is infused with elements of French Catholicism.

Overview of Hoodoo

While Santeria and Voodoo are generally considered religions, Hoodoo is often described as a folk spirituality. Hoodoo blends the traditional spiritual practices of various African tribes as they were brought over to America as a result of the Transatlantic Slave Trade. The center of Hoodoo practices revolves around ceremonies and rituals designed to access various supernatural forces in order to improve their lives. These ceremonies were thought to help the practitioner achieve power or success in various aspects of life such as love, healthy, money and employment.

Another important aspect of Hoodoo that overlaps to some degree with Santeria is an emphasis on contact with ancestors and various spirits of the dead. One point of difference is in the fact that Hoodoo can be practiced by anyone – ceremonies do not require a formally designated minister in the way that Santeria practices are overseen by priests, priestesses and elders. Some Hoodoo ceremonies also involve the reading of Psalms from the Bible – there is a certain degree of Christian influence in Hoodoo.

Chapter Six: Frequently Asked Questions

Q: *Where does Santeria come from?*

A: Santeria is an Afro-Caribbean religion originally practiced by the Yoruba people that grew out of the Cuban slave trade. It is primarily an oral tradition that is centered on various African traditions but parallels some aspects of Catholicism

Q: *Do followers of Santeria believe in God?*

A: Followers of Santeria believe in a supreme creator, Olorun, but the worship individual Orishas (lesser spiritual beings) who guide them toward their destiny. To curry favor with their Orishas, santeros give offerings and build altars in their homes.

Q: *Is Santeria the same as Voodoo or Hoodoo?*

A: All three of these religions are African-derived and they were heavily influenced by the slave trade. Many of the core principles of these religions are the same such as the worship of gods, the practice of ceremonies and rituals, and a belief in destiny. After leaving Africa, however, they received different influences – Santeria merged with aspects of Roman Catholicism, Voodoo became infused with aspects of French Catholicism, and Hoodoo took one some Christian influences.

Q: *How do I initiate into Santeria?*

A: Before you even think about initiating into Santeria you need to find a godparent who will help you learn about the religion and who will lead you through the divination process to see if initiation is part of your destiny. If it is, you will go through various ceremonies and rituals to identify and invoke your Orisha.

Q: *Why is Santeria such a secretive religion?*

A: The initial followers of Santeria came to the Americas during the slave trade and they were religiously prosecuted and forced to adopt Western religion. In an effort to retain some their traditions and values they merged their religion with aspects of Roman Catholicism.

Q: *Does everyone who initiates into Santeria become a priest?*

A: No, Santeria is a communal religion but each individual experiences it differently depending on their destiny. Some followers are destined to become initiated and to become priests and priestesses while others are destined to always be non-initiated followers.

Q: *Do Santeria followers believe in the devil?*

A: No, while Santeria followers believe in a supreme being or God (Olorun), they do not believe in an opposing force such as the devil. Santeria does recognize the individual's ability to do both harm and good, but there is no supreme negative force.

Q: *Does Santeria has some kind of religious text like the Bible?*

A: The Lukumi tradition is largely oral, passed down from one generation to the next by word of mouth. There are a variety of stories (patakis) and sayings (proverbs) that are commonly believed and spread but they are not all organized in a single text.

Q: *Do practitioners worship just one Orisha?*

A: During initiation, practitioners receive their head Orisha but they may also receive anywhere from 5 to 9 others. Each Orisha has its own ceremony and ritual.

Conclusion

By now you should have a deeper understanding of Santeria including its history and core concepts. As you have also learned, however, Santeria is a highly secretive religion so there is a great deal more to learn about it – especially if you are considering joining the religion. Rather than searching your local library for reference books or doing research online, your best bet to learn more about Santeria is to connect with a local church. Santeria is a religion that you can only learn through experience – you need a godparent to guide you.

Although Santeria is not the easiest religion to join, it does offer its practitioners many benefits that make it worthwhile. When you initiate into Santeria you become initiated to a particular Orisha who will help you to determine your destiny and the proper path your life should follow. In addition to giving your life meaning and direction, the Santeria religion also offers a strong community and support system. You may find that joining the Santeria religion gives you peace of mind and a purpose for your life.

So, if you are considering joining Santeria, take the time to find a local church and connect with its members in order to find someone willing to be your godparent, guiding you through the initiation process. The information in this book will give you a head start, but in the end Santeria is something you need to experience for yourself – it is not a religion for which words do justice.

Index

P

R

S

Photo Credits

Cover Photo by Flickr user Bistrosavage, <https://www.flickr.com/photos/bistrosavage/15426201/sizes/l>

Page 1 Photo Purchased from BigStockPhoto.com

Page 6 Photo Purchased from BigStockPhoto.com

Page 7 Photo by Susanne Bollinger via Wikimedia Commons, <https://commons.wikimedia.org/wiki/File:SB090_Santer%C3%ADa_altar.JPG>

Page 9 Photo by Jorge Royan via Wikimedia Commons, <https://commons.wikimedia.org/wiki/File:Havana_-_Cuba_-_0583.jpg>

Page 11 Photo by Bernardo Capellini via Wikimedia Commons, <https://commons.wikimedia.org/wiki/File:Santeria_Centro_Habana.JPG>

Page 14 Photo Purchased from BigStockPhoto.com

Page 39 Photo by Flickr user Vince Alongi, <https://www.flickr.com/photos/vincealongi/298472382/sizes/o/>

Page 41 Photo Purchased from BigStockPhoto.com

Page 44 Photo by Flickr user Jaumescar, <https://www.flickr.com/photos/jaumescar/8707656966/sizes/l>

Page 45 Photo by Flickr user Giumaiolini, <https://www.flickr.com/photos/giumaiolini/470247792/sizes/o/>

Page 47 Photo by Flickr user Bruce Tuten, <https://www.flickr.com/photos/savannahgrandfather/6928892699/sizes/l>

Page 51 Photo by Ji-Elle via Wikimedia Commons, <https://commons.wikimedia.org/wiki/File:La_Havane-Vente_d%27articles_religieux-Santer%C3%ADa_(4).jpg>

Page 54 11 Photo by Flickr user Datospersonales, <https://www.flickr.com/photos/datospersonales/6076221339/sizes/o/>

Page 55 Photo by Calvin Hennick via Wikimedia Commons, <https://en.wikipedia.org/wiki/Haitian_Vodou#/media/File: Haitian_vodou_altar_to_Petwo,_Rada,_and_Gede_spirits;_ November_5,_2010..jpg>

Page 58 Photo by Flickr user Nimdok, <https://www.flickr.com/photos/nimdok/8405150635/sizes/l>

Page 62 Photo by Flickr user Benkucinski, <https://www.flickr.com/photos/kucinski/10548429785/>

References

"A Taste of Lucumi Proverbs." HubPages. <http://hubpages.com/religion-philosophy/A-Taste-of-Lucumi-Proverbs>

"Advice to Newcomers to Orisha Worship." Wemba-Music.org. <http://www.wemba-music.org/advice_to_newcomers.htm>

"An Initiation to Santeria in Cuba." HavanaTimes. <http://www.havanatimes.org/?p=105400>

Armas, Daniela. "Things You Should Know About Santeria." Latino Life. <http://www.latinolife.co.uk/node/231>

"Beliefs and Practices." ReligiousTolerance.org. <http://www.religioustolerance.org/santeri3.htm>

"FAQ Lukumi Santeria." Wemba-Music.org. <http://www.wemba-music.org/orisha_faq.htm>

"How to Learn Santeria – Studying the Religion." Santeria Church of the Orishas. <http://santeriachurch.org/how-to-learn-santeria/>

"Initiation in La Regla Ocha (Santeria)." OrishaNet.org. <http://www.orishanet.org/initiate.html>

"Initiations." Santeria Church of the Orishas. <http://santeriachurch.org/our-services/santeria-initiations/>

"Orishas." Santeria Church of the Orishas. <http://santeriachurch.org/the-orishas/>

Pichardo, Oba Ernesto. "Santeria in Contemporary Cuba: The Individual Life and Condition of the Priesthood." The Church of the Lukumi Babalu Aye. <http://www.churchofthelukumi.com/santeria-in-contemporary-cuba.html>

"Santeria." Encyclopedia Britannica. <https://www.britannica.com/topic/Santeria>

"Santeria." Types of Religion. <http://www.typesofreligion.com/santeria.html>

"Terminology: Number & Location of Followers." ReligiousTolerance.org. <http://www.religioustolerance.org/santeri2.htm>

"The Growth of Santeria." BBC.co.uk. <http://www.bbc.co.uk/religion/religions/santeria/history/growth.shtml>

Tolentino, Jia. "Interview with a Santeria Priestess." The Hairpin. <https://thehairpin.com/interview-with-a-santeria-priestess-78cd8df4ac7d>

"What is the Difference Between Voodoo, Hoodoo, and Santeria?" Santeria Church of the Orishas.

<http://santeriachurch.org/what-is-the-difference-between-voodoo-hoodoo-and-santeria/>

"Why is it Called Santeria?" AboutSanteria. <http://www.aboutsanteria.com/what-is-santeria.html>

Feeding Baby
Cynthia Cherry
978-1941070000

Axolotl
Lolly Brown
978-0989658430

Dysautonomia, POTS
Syndrome
Frederick Earlstein
978-0989658485

Degenerative Disc
Disease Explained
Frederick Earlstein
978-0989658485

Sinusitis, Hay Fever,
Allergic Rhinitis Explained
Frederick Earlstein
978-1941070024

Wicca
Riley Star
978-1941070130

Zombie Apocalypse
Rex Cutty
978-1941070154

Capybara
Lolly Brown
978-1941070062

Eels As Pets
Lolly Brown
978-1941070167

Scabies and Lice Explained
Frederick Earlstein
978-1941070017

Saltwater Fish As Pets
Lolly Brown
978-0989658461

Torticollis Explained
Frederick Earlstein
978-1941070055

Kennel Cough
Lolly Brown
978-0989658409

Physiotherapist, Physical
Therapist
Christopher Wright
978-0989658492

Rats, Mice, and Dormice
As Pets
Lolly Brown
978-1941070079

Wallaby and Wallaroo Care
Lolly Brown
978-1941070031

Bodybuilding Supplements
Explained
Jon Shelton
978-1941070239

Demonology
Riley Star
978-19401070314

Pigeon Racing
Lolly Brown
978-1941070307

Dwarf Hamster
Lolly Brown
978-1941070390

Cryptozoology
Rex Cutty
978-1941070406

Eye Strain
Frederick Earlstein
978-1941070369

Inez The Miniature Elephant
Asher Ray
978-1941070353

Vampire Apocalypse
Rex Cutty
978-1941070321

Made in United States
North Haven, CT
09 January 2023

30850530R00049